---

is learning how to write numbers!

one

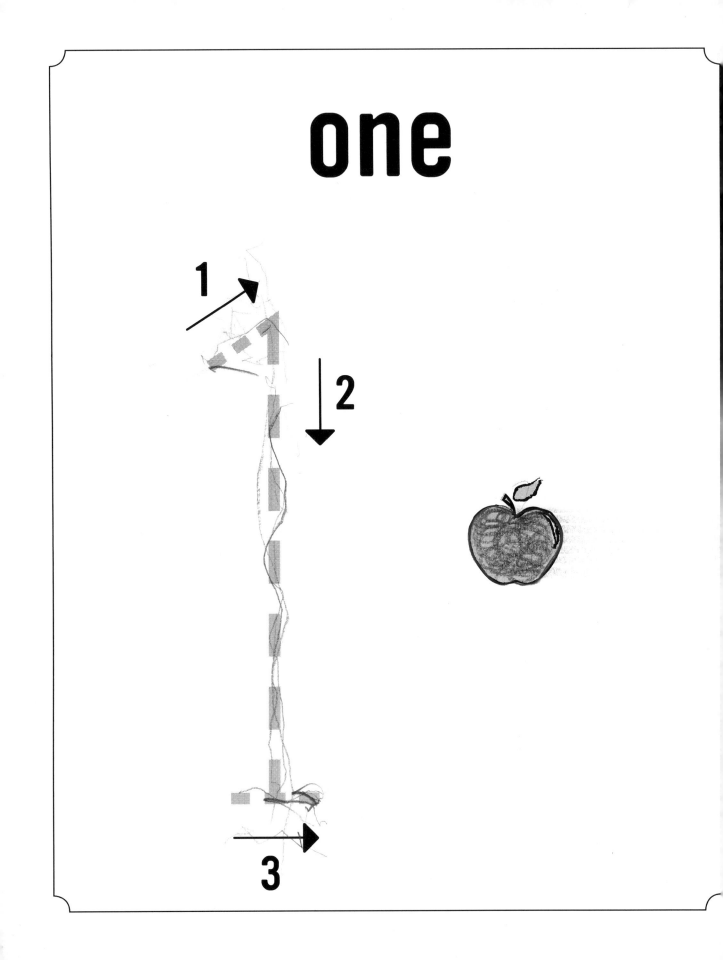

Now it's time to practice!

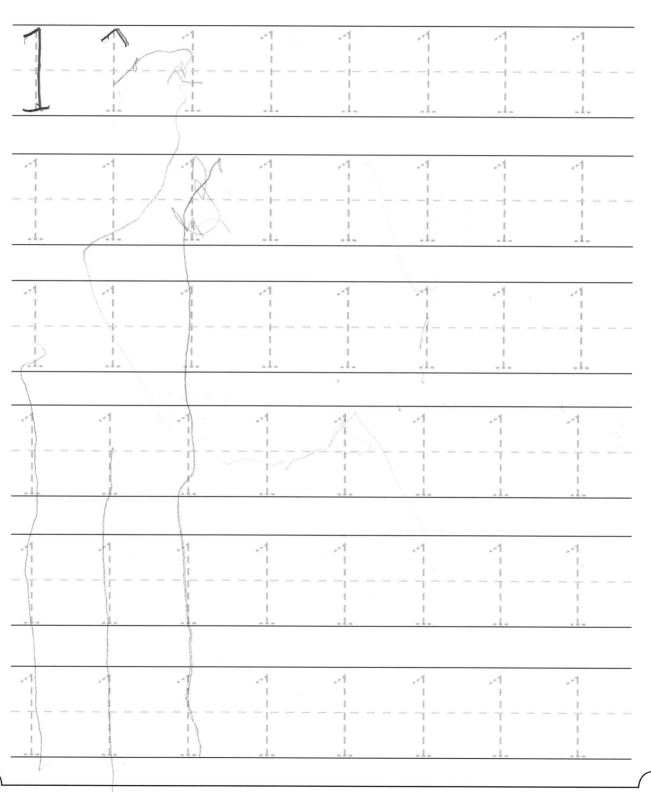

1 1 1 1 1 1 1 1

1 1 1 1 1 1 1 1

1 1 1 1 1 1 1 1

1 1 1 1 1 1 1 1

1 1 1 1 1 1 1 1

1 1 1 1 1 1 1 1

1 1 1 1 1 1 1 1

1 1 1 1 1 1 1 1

1 1 1 1 1 1 1 1

1 1 1 1 1 1 1 1

1 1 1 1 1 1 1 1

1 1 1 1 1 1 1 1

1 1 1 1 1 1 1 1

1 1 1 1 1 1 1 1

1 1 1 1 1 1 1 1

1 1 1 1 1 1 1 1

1 1 1 1 1 1 1 1

1 1 1 1 1 1 1

This page is a little harder. Try your best to follow the numbers as they get lighter!

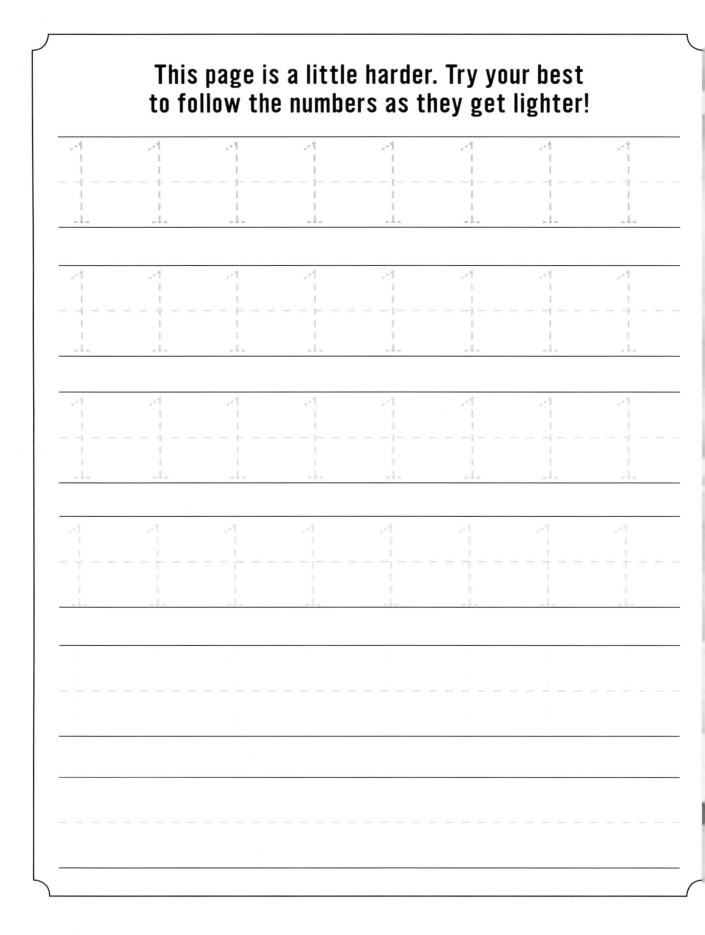

two

Now it's time to practice!

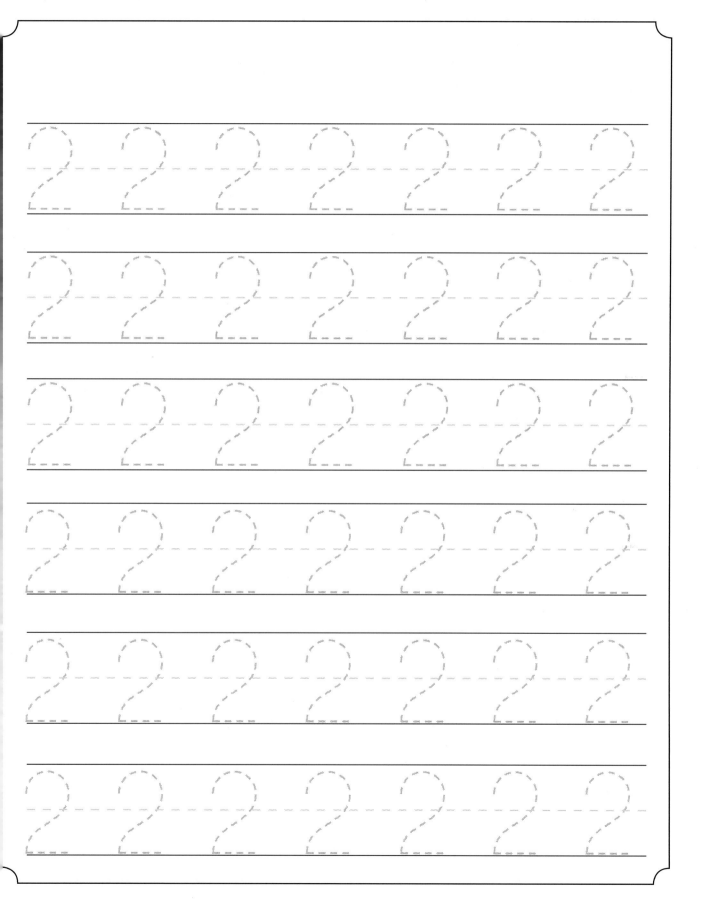

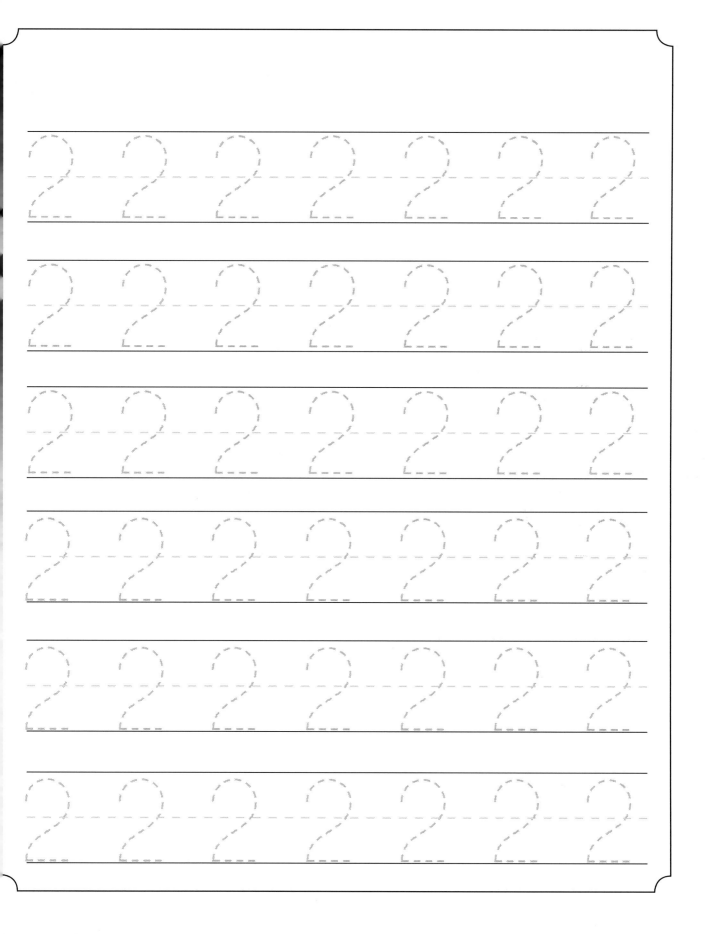

This page is a little harder. Try your best to follow the numbers as they get lighter!

three

Now it's time to practice!

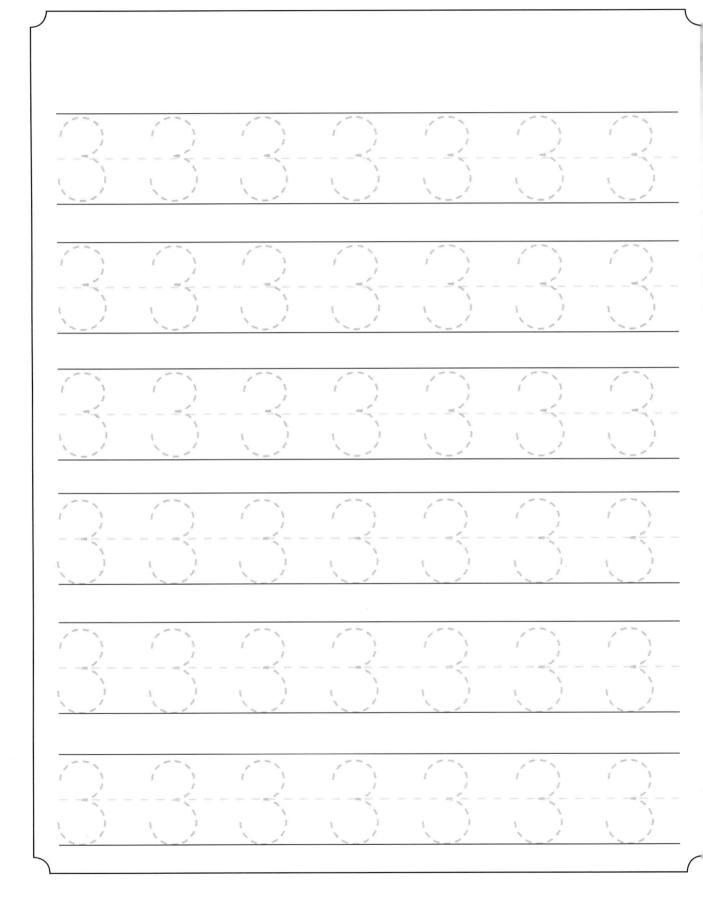

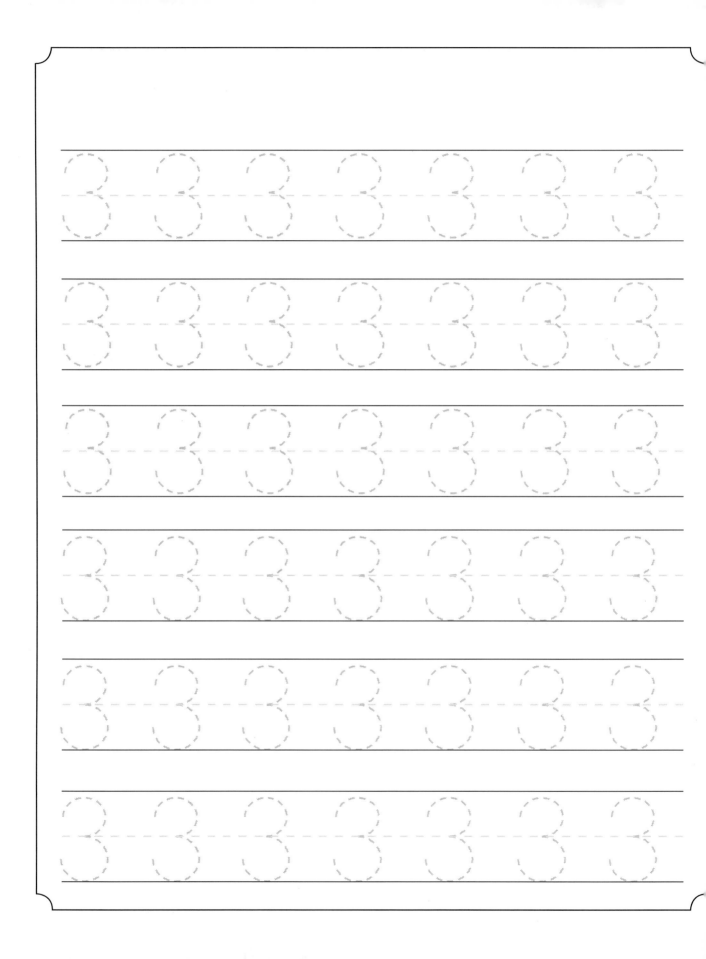

This page is a little harder. Try your best to follow the numbers as they get lighter!

four

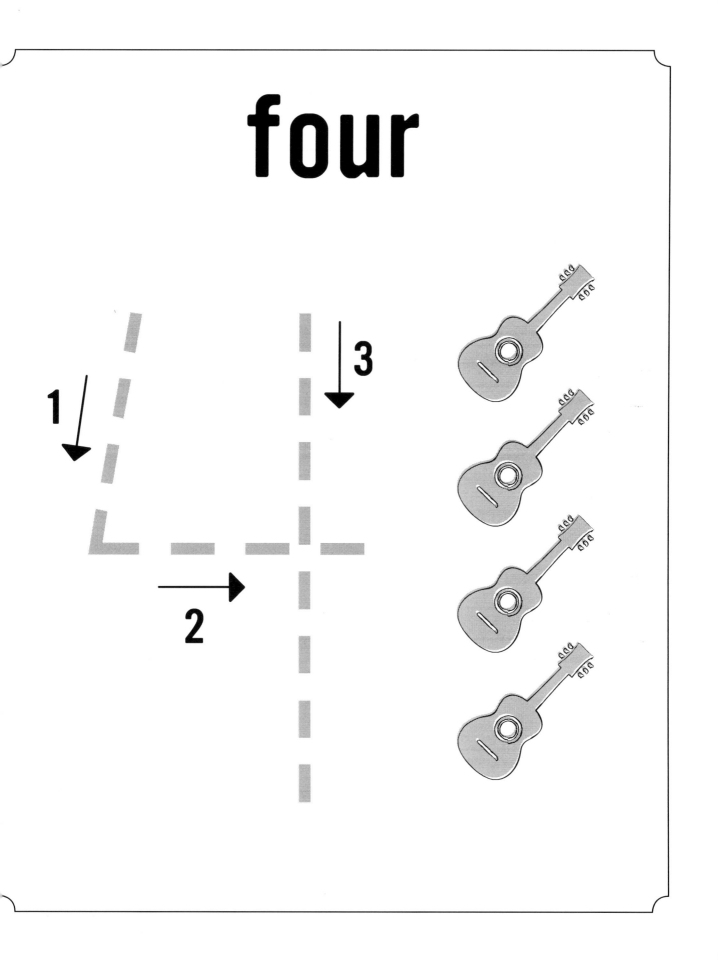

Now it's time to practice!

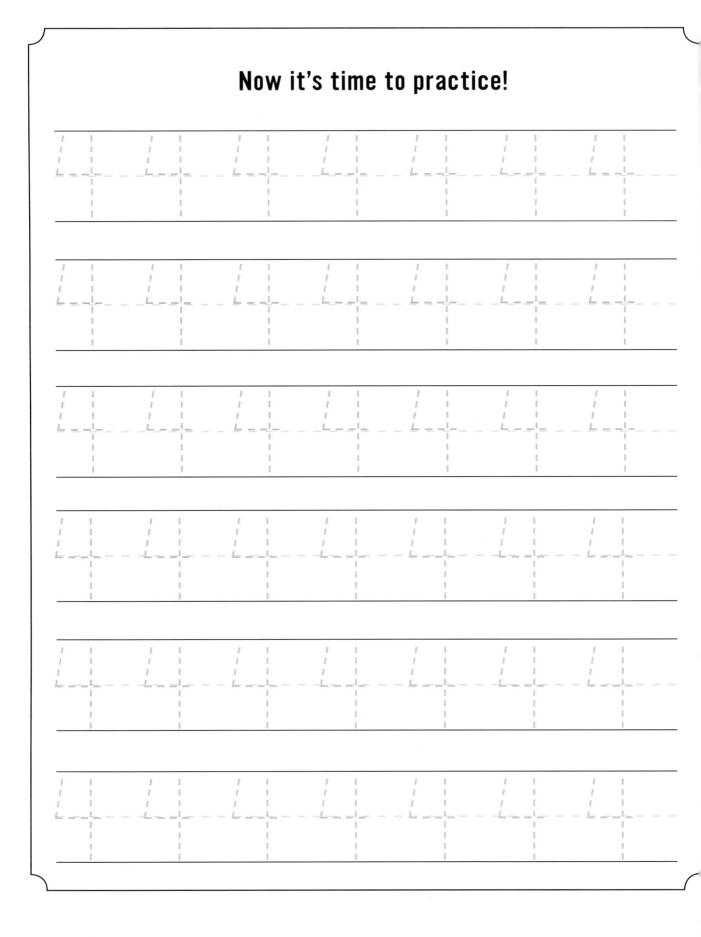

This page is a little harder. Try your best to follow the numbers as they get lighter!

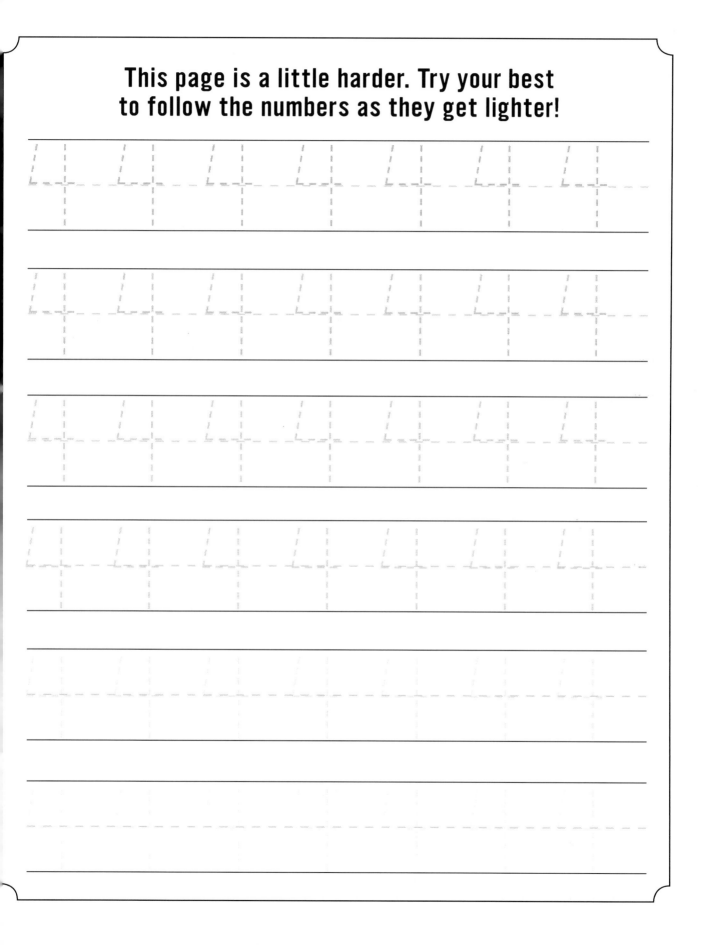

five

Now it's time to practice!

5 5 5 5 5 5 5

5 5 5 5 5 5 5

5 5 5 5 5 5 5

5 5 5 5 5 5 5

5 5 5 5 5 5 5

5 5 5 5 5 5 5

5 5 5 5 5 5 5

5 5 5 5 5 5 5

5 5 5 5 5 5 5

5 5 5 5 5 5 5

5 5 5 5 5 5 5

5 5 5 5 5 5 5

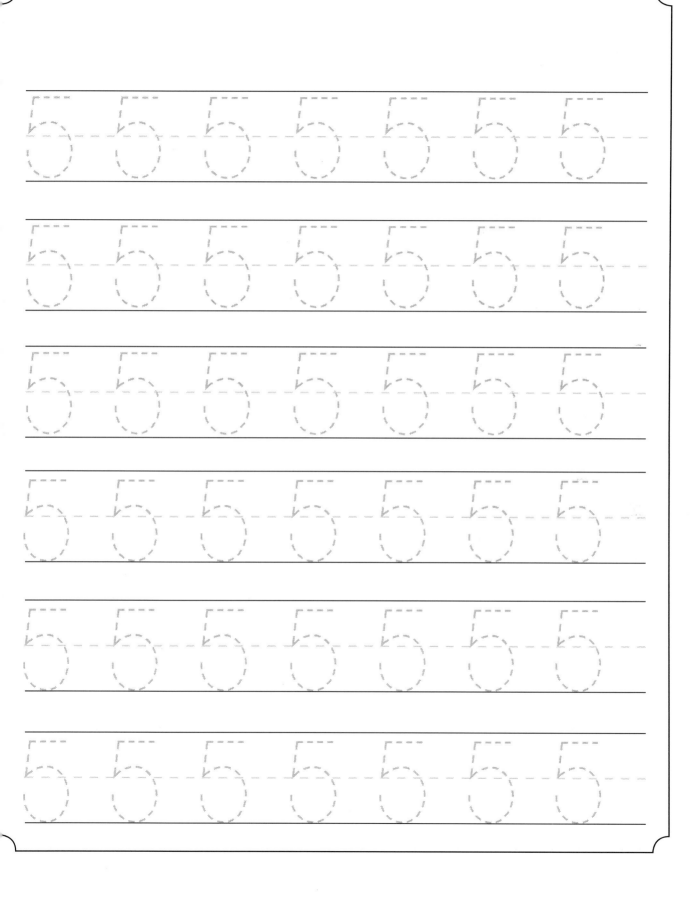

5 5 5 5 5 5 5
5 5 5 5 5 5 5
5 5 5 5 5 5 5
5 5 5 5 5 5 5
5 5 5 5 5 5 5
5 5 5 5 5 5 5

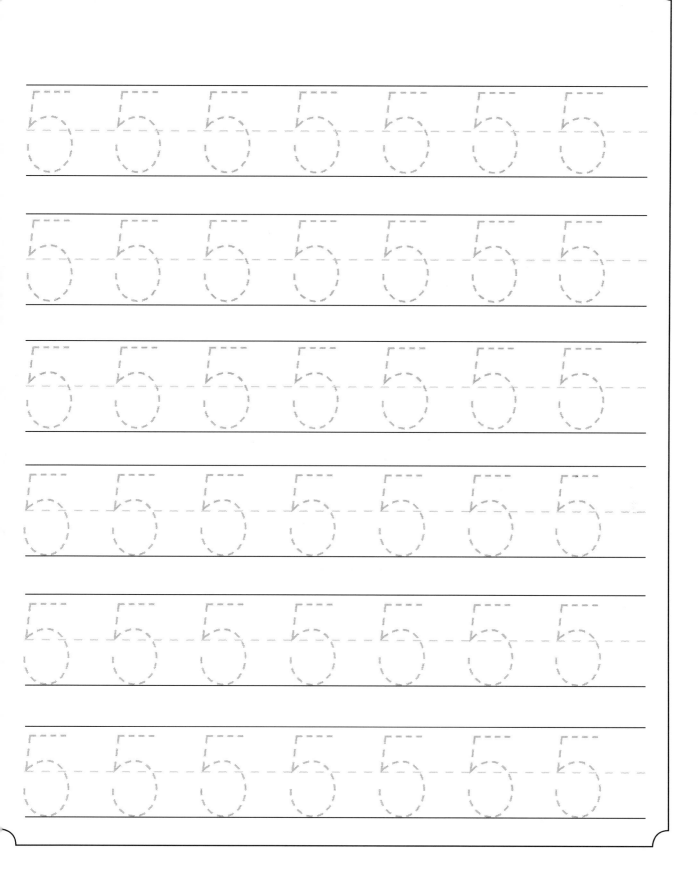

This page is a little harder. Try your best to follow the numbers as they get lighter!

six

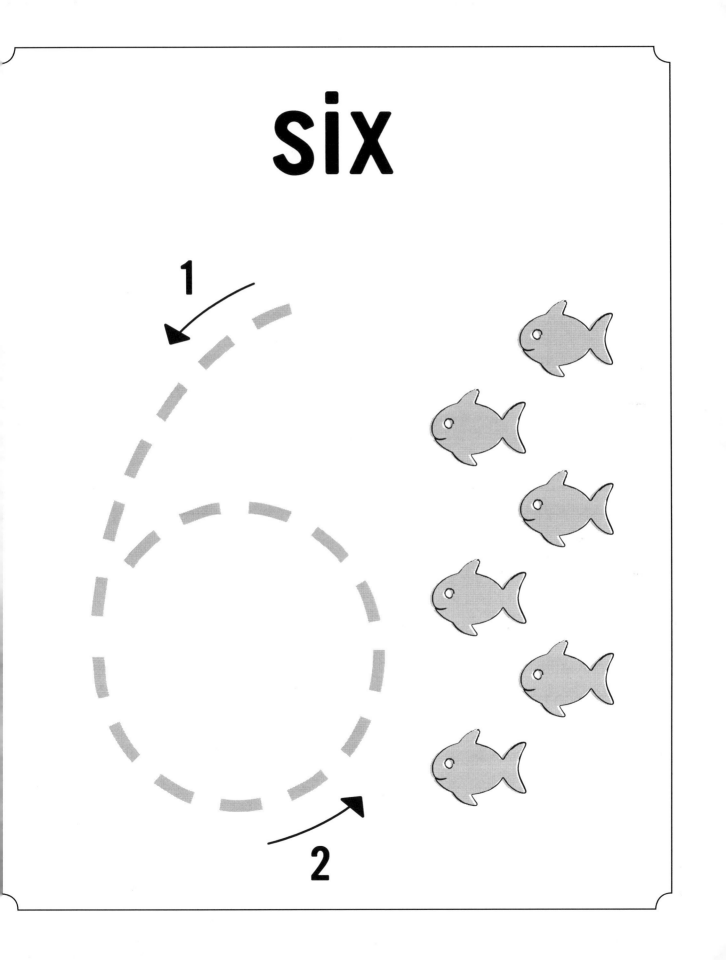

Now it's time to practice!

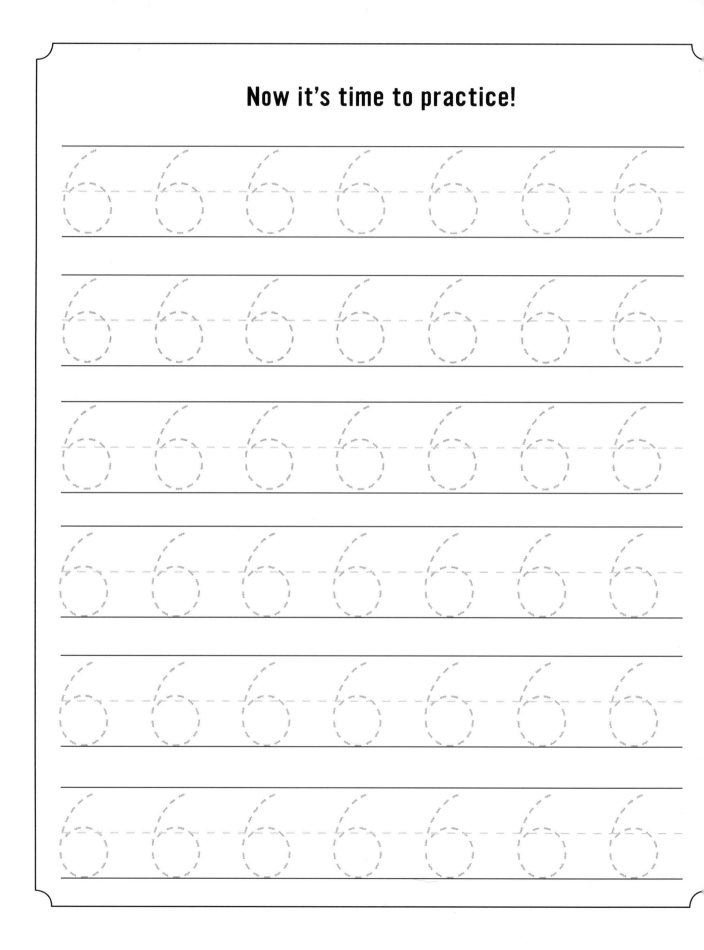

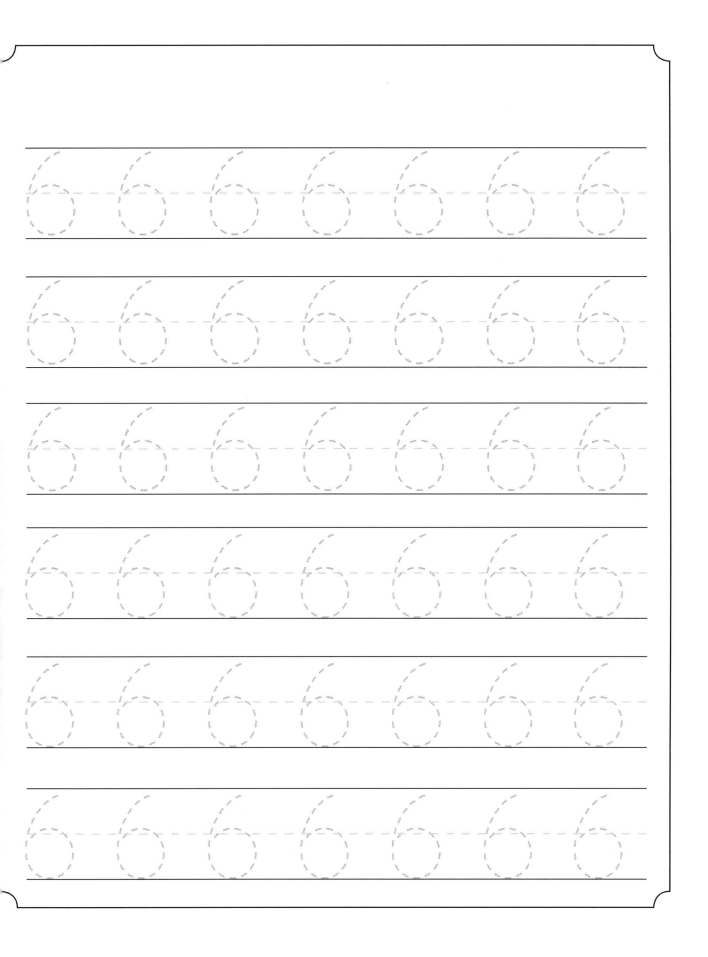

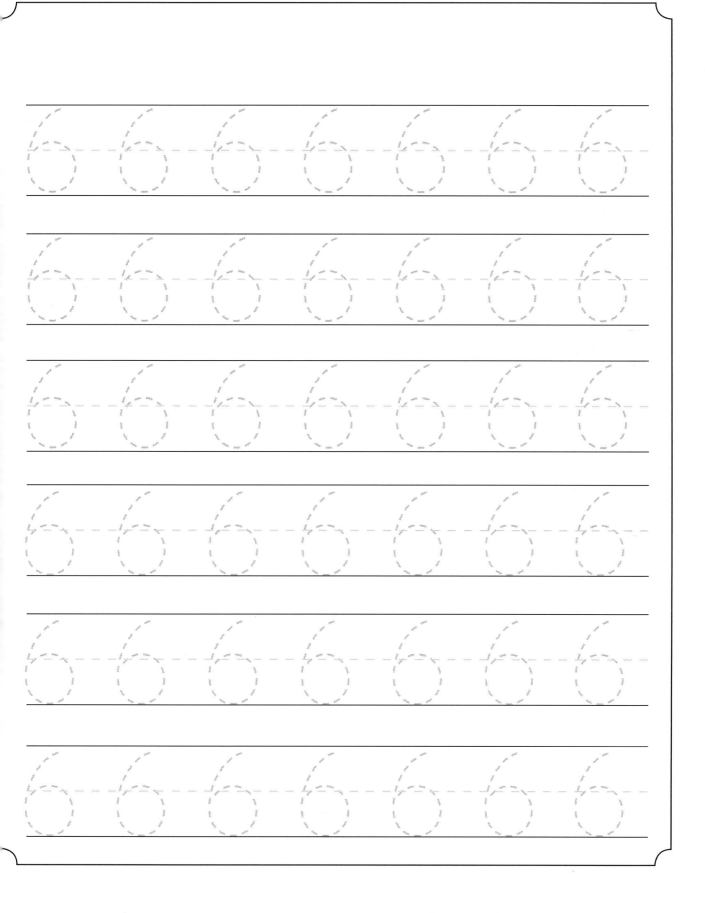

This page is a little harder. Try your best to follow the numbers as they get lighter!

seven

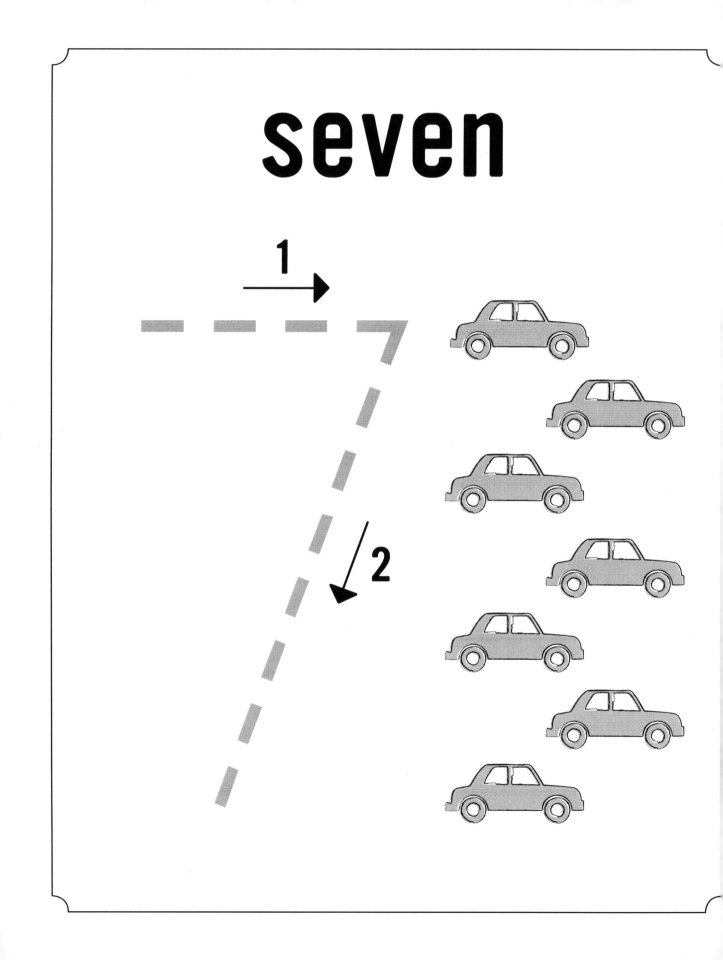

Now it's time to practice!

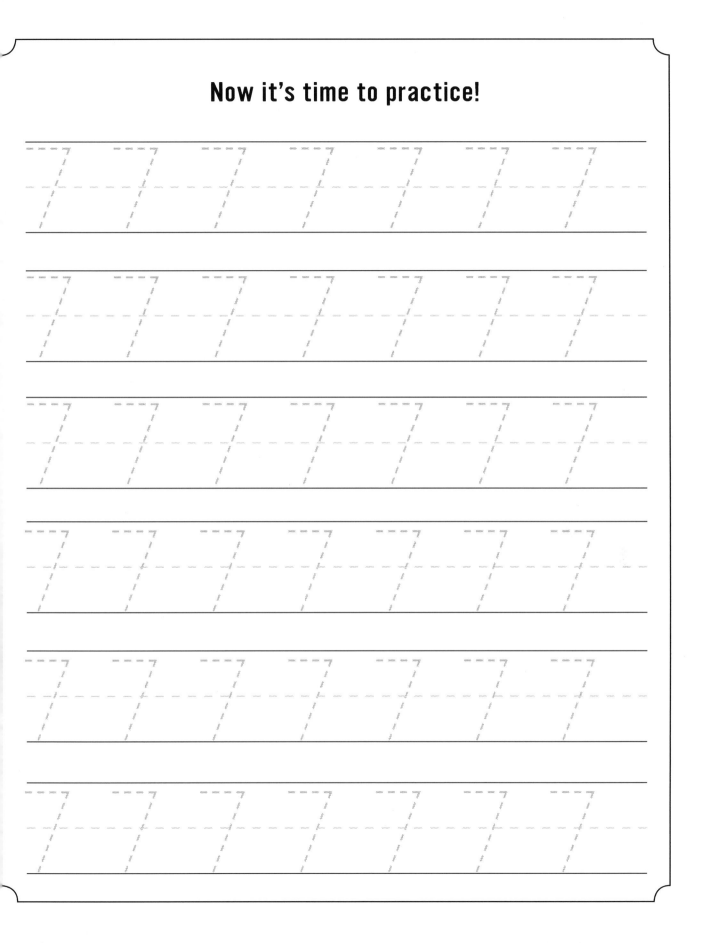

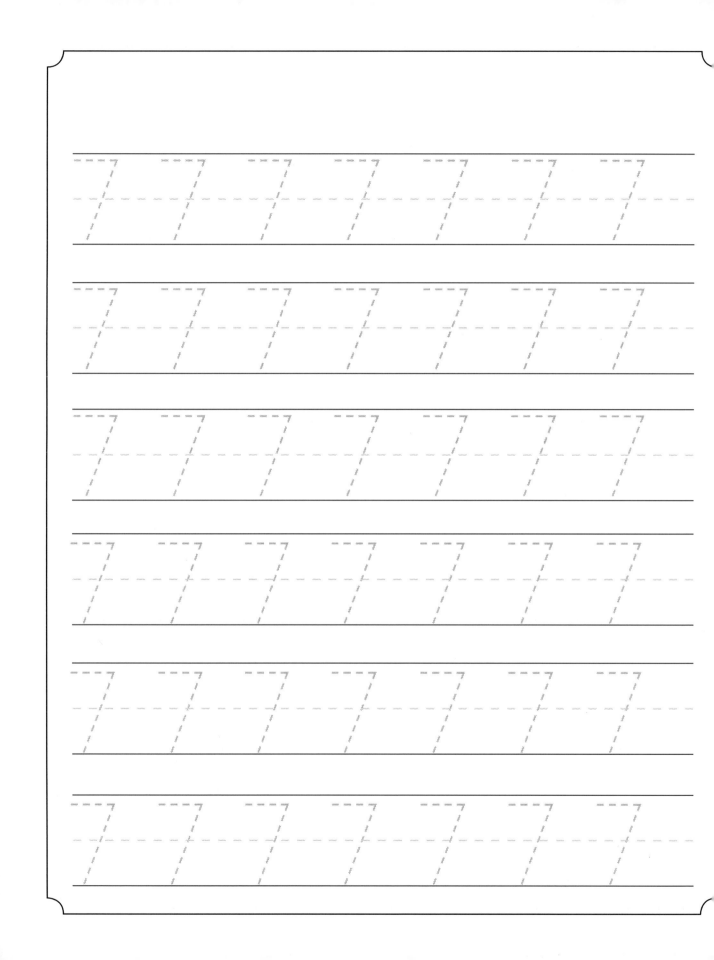

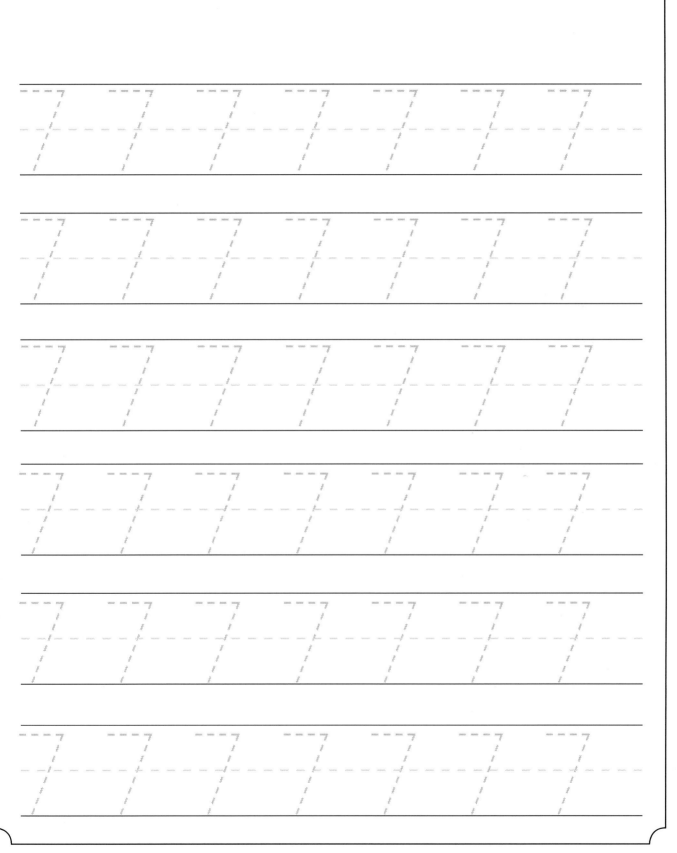

This page is a little harder. Try your best to follow the numbers as they get lighter!

eight

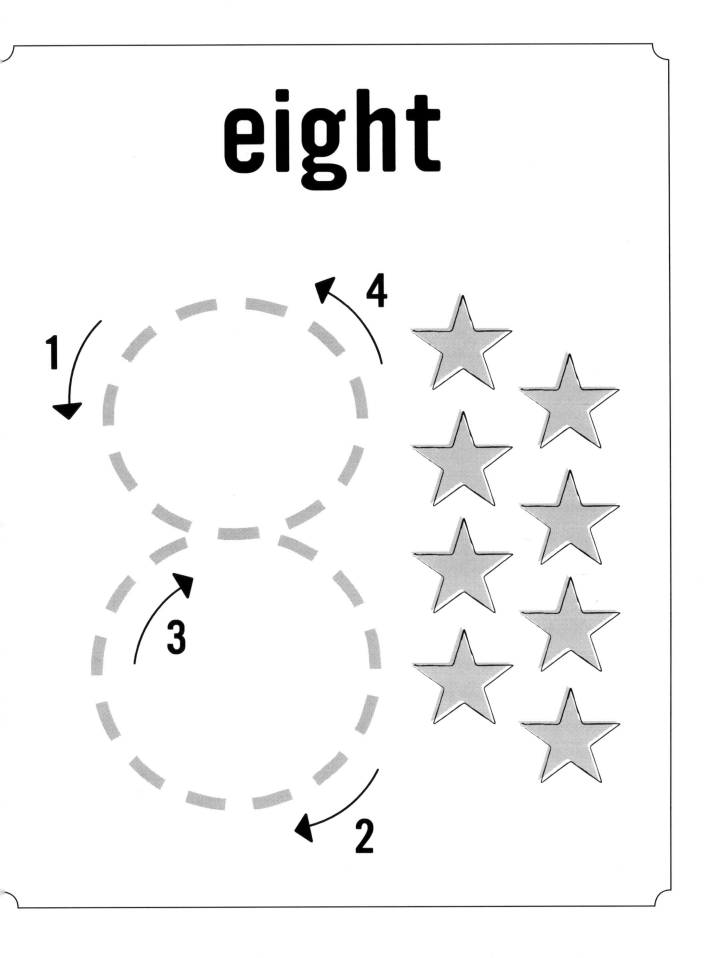

Now it's time to practice!

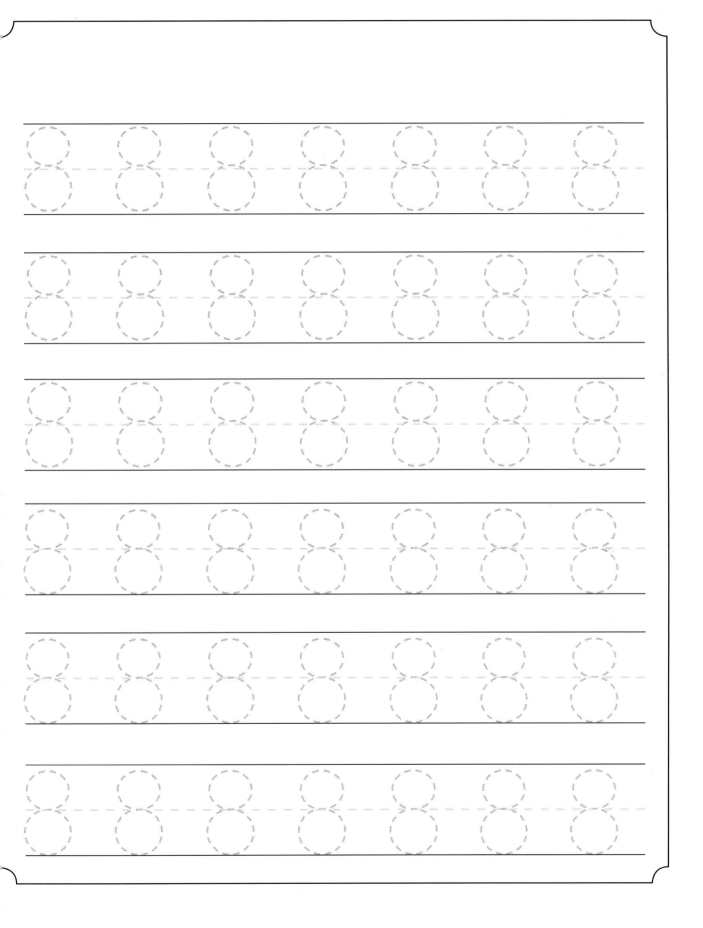

This page is a little harder. Try your best to follow the numbers as they get lighter!

nine

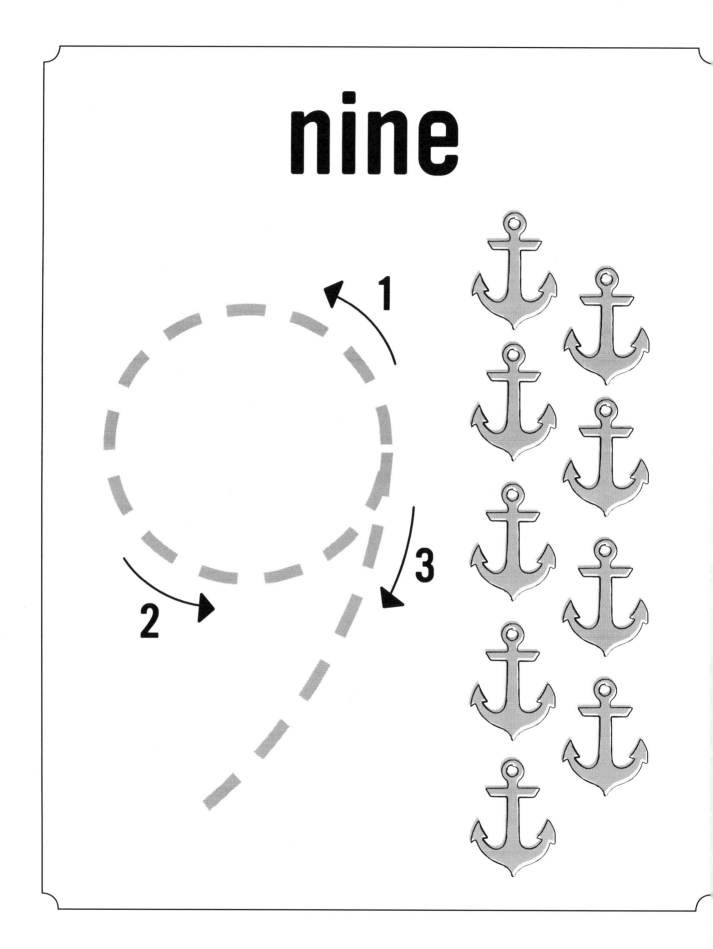

Now it's time to practice!

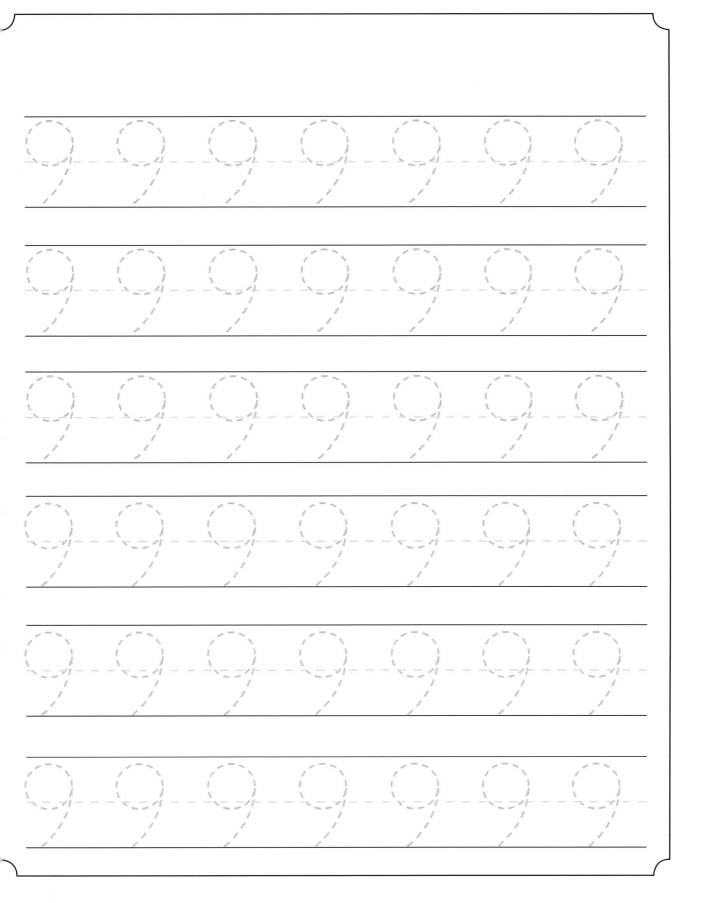

This page is a little harder. Try your best to follow the numbers as they get lighter!

zero

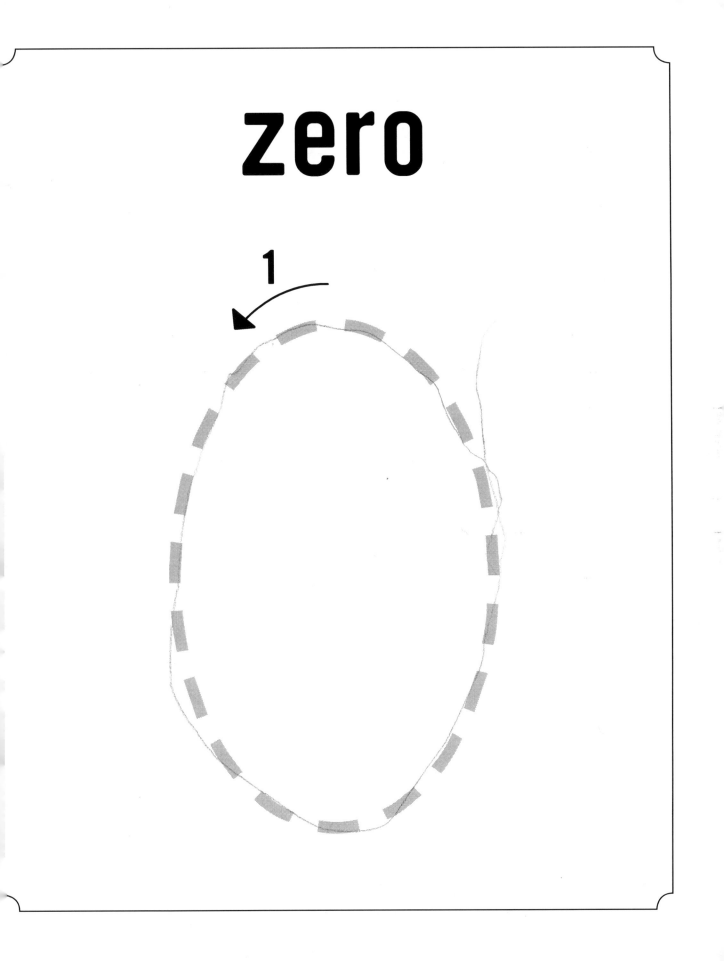

Now it's time to practice!

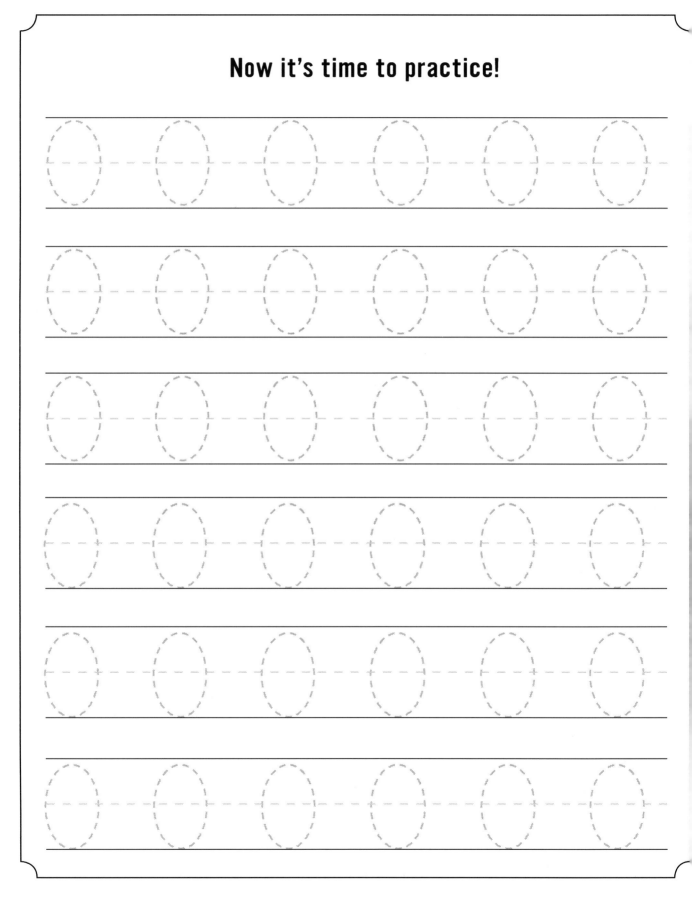

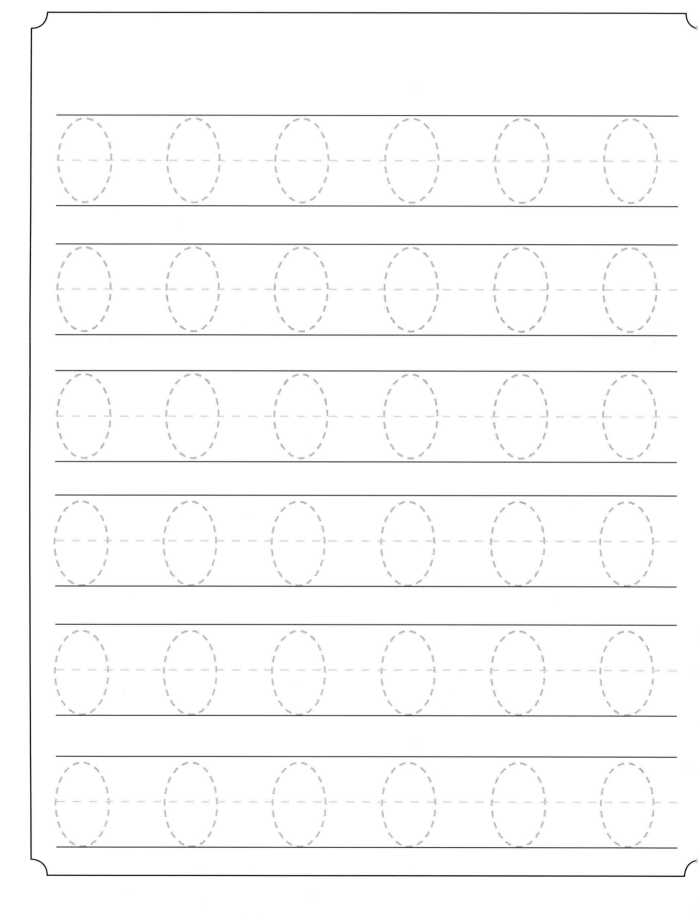

This page is a little harder. Try your best to follow the numbers as they get lighter!

Made in the USA
Middletown, DE
14 September 2017